Salvage

BOOKS BY MICHAEL CRUMMEY

FICTION
Flesh & Blood (stories)
River Thieves

POETRY
Arguments with Gravity
Hard Light
Emergency Roadside Assistance (chapbook)
Salvage

Salvage

MICHAEL CRUMMEY

M&S

National Library of Canada Cataloguing in Publication Data

Crummey, Michael
Salvage

Poems.
ISBN 0-7710-2471-1

I. Title.

PS8555.R84S24 2002   C811'.54   C2001-903829-1
PR9199.3.C717S24 2002

We acknowledge the financial support of the Government of Canada through the Book Publishing Industry Development Program for our publishing activities. We further acknowledge the support of the Canada Council for the Arts and the Ontario Arts Council for our publishing program.

Text design by Sean Tai
Typeset in Sabon by M&S, Toronto
Printed and bound in Canada

McClelland & Stewart Ltd.
The Canadian Publishers
481 University Ave.
Toronto, Ontario
M5G 2E9
www.mcclelland.com

1 2 3 4 5   06 05 04 03 02

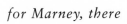

for Marney, there

CONTENTS

KISSING THE DEAD: A DISCLAIMER

For years now he's been telling people
he's writing a sad book,
a book about loss,
as if he feels some sort of
notice is necessary,
a public warning.

Sad Book Ahead.

Poems about Loss
    Next 100 pgs.

Thinks of the friend who was carted
to wakes as a girl,
lifted above coffin-sills to kiss
a succession of ancient strangers
she couldn't even name.
Appalled by it now,
the vellum feel of the skin,
the fact she wasn't given a choice.
What was the point of that?
she wants to know,
and he can't fashion a sensible answer
or shake the feeling he's just
setting things down on paper
to leave them there,
gaping like potholes.

Pointing them out as people go by.

Saying something as useless as
Mind your step.

APPARATUS

Two moths pitched on the white
of a page left under lamplight,
sleek and symmetrical
in the margins of the text
like components of some apparatus
ancient and esoteric as poetry,
stilled antennae and the long
dusk-coloured cloak of wings,
both so watchful they seem
almost inanimate

Touch the paper and they're up
storming the bare light,
nearly translucent against the glass
and fierce
       fierce

THREE LANDSCAPES

1
Slack water –
the unbroken silence of
prairie at noon lethargic as
the tide before it turns,
land falling away in all directions,
an emptiness not even light
can fill

      moon just visible
on the horizon
pale fish eye,
white thumbprint on glass

2

Minke whales in the salt water
of the Sound,
the soft chuff of exhalation when they surface
dark as roses,
their backs smudged by moonlight;
beach stones at our feet
ground smooth by the ocean's long finger,
mountains rising into mist
above us

      slow pull of the tide
at their roots

3
Night's flat prairie –
moon in the crook of gravity's elbow,
pocked face as full
as a sunflower;
stars drifting behind it like
seeds on the wind,
the moon blind to their dance,
to their sudden implosions,
deaf to the soft chuff
of exhalation as a star expires

       light falling away
in all directions

Heading for a cheap-beer-on-tap
greasy spoon at College and Bathurst
he passes a man with his hand out,
practised nonchalance, expecting nothing
to cheat disappointment.
The sky above them so faded
it's barely legible, a battalion
of yellow street lights feeding
on the tender shoots of constellations.

He's brought an old edition of
The New American Poets,
sips his way through two pints,
through Kerouac and Ginsberg,
their cities alive in those lines
like ugly flowers in a waterglass
and both of them dead now,
Monday Night Football on
television over the bar –
brute force veined with strategies
so intricate the game looks
almost graceful from a distance,
the remote choreography of stars.

The book holding its hands
out to the air like the small
perfect leaves of a tree
feeding on sunlight.

DOSTOEVSKY

A single set of steel rails
translates the trackless Gobi
into something comprehensible,
slow train travelling west to east
like a finger following a line of print.

Days and nights the same flat quarry
of broken stone out the window,
packed cars full of the desert's heat,
the clutter of Mandarin conversations,
hollow time he feeds
with *The Brothers Karamazov*,
a hand on the knotted line
unspooled by Dostoevsky,
his pale face blank with attention.

An old man leans in to lift the novel
from his hands, inspecting the cover,
riffling the leaves of print as if judging
the quality of a harvest crop.
Returns the book with a shrug,
disappointed somehow, his weathered face
dark and inscrutable as a Russian winter.

The train sways on the rails like a voice
holding and holding a single note,
the desert leans in the window
muttering its stark indecipherable language.

WHORE

Evenings you take your place
beside the churchyard fence across the street,
thumbing into the slow river of traffic
as if all you were hitching was a lift,
everything else about you pitched
an octave above its natural range,
like a runner wired on adrenaline,
like a living thing impaled on a hook.
Bare limbs wasted by your body's
corrosive habit, joints swollen
like knots in bamboo,
your angular face so tortured
wanting one thing
it is almost blank.

A shoal of boys cruising the old cemetery before dark
hiss insults behind headstones –
their word for you is a dark well they stare into,
little cocks barbed and snagging
in the cotton folds of their underwear.
They have no idea why they despise you.

You stand there long after those boys
have taken you to their beds,
bruised by the street lamp's purple,
thumb dangling like bait in
the bright stream of headlights.
The dark church leans over the street
like a face watching a spider at work,

waiting to see which passing stranger
will take your line and reel you in.

HOW HE CARRIED IT

It hovered in the boy's head pale
as a daylight moon

It lit him up like a field
under a hail of lightning,
it torched the buildings locked
and almost hidden under brush
in the unfenced backyard of his mind

It travelled in his blood like blooms
of silt stirred from a river bottom,
it ticked like a clock toward
some alarm his body
lay awake for,
it made him feel ancient and
unrecoverable and lonely
for his friends

It churned inside him
like the crankshaft of the planet,
darkness endlessly turning
toward a deeper darkness
he had no name for

It settled on him like squatters
claiming farmland lying fallow,
like summer dusk staining
the distant hills blue

UNDONE

I want you to tie me up.

It was very late,
even the moon was asleep.

He tied her up.

Her face in the tight halo of
light from the bedside clock,
hands crossed at the wrists
behind her back.

Tell me what you want.

Her smile then,
the sudden tug of it,
like a knot being
tested.

It was very late,
the stars about to be undone
by daylight.

After he slipped her hands free
she held him awhile,
could see he needed comforting.

A slow heat rising from
her skin where she touched him,
like the sun
about to come up.

POMEGRANATE

She turned from the table,
lifted the dark red seed to
his mouth, her body having already
made up her mind –
     bright stain on her skin,
fingertips a row of
small wounds

Sudden bouquet of flavour
suddenly wilting
     and then the salt his mouth
took from her hand,
as if she were already cut
by the sadness that follows
the body's blind wanting,
the familiar aftertaste
of regret

*There's that pit at the core
of sweetness* she might have said,
gathering another clutch of seed
from the ruined star of fruit
     and tasting it herself

DRIFTWOOD

Gathering for the greedy fire

Crooked limbs tangled among beach grass,
bone-white and brittle,
last gestures of birch,
blue spruce and larch
stripped of bark
by lake water and rain

Dry, almost weightless,
nearly cured
of the world's heft

All afternoon the fire's interrogation:
flames fingering
each naked spine
as if learning
an alphabet in Braille

Gnarled branches of smoke
drift in the clear air

BLIND WILLIE JOHNSON

Blinded at age seven by a spiteful fist of lye,
the water he'd hoped would ease the burn flared
like a match to kerosene, scorching the panes of his eyes,
turning them inward like this cottage window at night,
trimmed wick of the lamp twinned in the dark square
with the old-fashioned wicker furniture,
like a sepia photo of a southern porch, circa 1928.

Blind Willie's voice chafes over the gas-light hiss
of those old recordings like rope against skin,
scarred by that burn, the ache still in it,
night sky raw with the corrosion of stars.
His words look to salvation from the world's darkness
but the music bickers with that promise,
gospel fired and hammered on the anvil of the blues,
prayers with a pocket-knife slide on the strings.

Dawn will flush the scald of stars from the sky,
a new morning will clear the window's blindness,
but nothing tomorrow brings will soothe that vibrato
left-hand slide, that voice bearing the weight
of a life lived black on the streets of Atlanta,
the waver of each note a kind of anguish,
embers kindling in a breeze,
dark blisters of light.

JAR OF BLUES

for TM

Remember how it used to be with us, lover,
every song you taught me,
every line

You on the stairs outside my door past dark,
weightless buzz climbing
the steps of my spine

Remember how greedy I was
to have you sugar
my mouth with honey

Days were nothing but hurt
after nights like that
Sunlight just made me lonely

Morning head ringing
like a jar of bees,
like John Lee Hooker singing
I messed around and fell in love

Well, well

Sick of being myself and nothing more
This could be a song for you
if you'd come up those stairs this evening

touch your hand to my door

CARRY THE ONE

Talk exhausted for the night
he walks her home in silence,
comes back to the small wreck
of the meal, empty containers, food scraps,
dishes stacked beside the sink
like beads on an abacus reckoning
an emotional failure's tired repetition.
Equations that map the stars turn
in and in on themselves like prayers
sieved and refined until symbol = value
but a life bogs down in simple arithmetic.
He's never known more than
what he doesn't want from the world,
division, subtraction, carry the one.

Half an hour later the plates gleam
in the rack like children fresh from a bath,
the upturned glasses like a wiser man's metaphor
for enlightenment, clarity and emptiness,
denial of the calculating self.
He turns out the light, counts the stairs
to his room, the necklace of stars framed
by the window over the bed.
He has never felt lonelier,
never so completely at home in his life.

A DOOR IS AJAR

He hooks a door shut in an unfamiliar house
that he recognizes as the home he shared with
a woman years ago, before he believed
himself capable of hurting anyone.
Walks through the building to find sinister
notes scattered on tables and desks upstairs
and down, all written by the door,
all threatening to do him injury
if the catch isn't unlocked.

In the morning he turns the dream over in
his mind, leafing through it like a paper
reporting old news, harm done and done with,
recalls confronting the door to accuse it
of siding with her –
shakes his head at that, how ludicrous,
how unaccountably terrified he was
when he woke.

Recounts the details as a sad joke to friends
who insist on paraphrasing Jung,
dream as metaphor, sly prophecy,
the dreamer's strange self leeching out of darkness –
stumbles upon it weeks later, illuminated
with borrowed light at the end of a hallway,
the closed door familiar, inscrutable,
like a lover's face shadowed
by contempt.

ALE & BITTER

Your days a deliberate
measured excursion into loss.
Cigarettes disappearing from
the pack at your elbow,
three pale soldiers
to every pint of ale or bitter,
glasses emptied and set aside
like spent cartridges,
wet butt of each hour
stubbed and tossed.
Your fingers stained the same stale
shade as the indoor light
that never changes:
sullen, nicotine, yellow.

A resolute, determined quitter,
pace steady as a metronome,
the copper facing around the bar
offers your reflection
in nostalgic sepia tone,
as if to say you're already most
of the way gone from here,
someone else's recollection.
Same forced march every night,
no variation, no turning.

You must hate to wake up
in the morning.

DETOUR

The bird's clerical black
glares like a harsh light against
a fall of new snow on the lake,
its beak crowbarring a meal
from the flesh of some dead thing
on the ice

Skirt the scavenger's mess
in my heavy boots,
the crow pausing to watch
without looking in my direction,
a fulcrum of oblique attention
in the afternoon silence:

the mutilated creature at its feet/
                        my careful detour

Heavy rain and water sluicing
the dark cartography of sewers
flushed two of them into daylight,
their dart across hardwood
lifting our knees to our chests,
hearts skittering wildly,
blood rattling through arteries
like rodents trapped in
a laboratory maze,
till panic translated to fury,
fear and revulsion parading
in a rational uniform,
carting an ancient list of crimes:
pestilence, disease, nocturnal theft.
We divided the kitchen into quarters,
ferreted under every article
of furniture, beneath every box and crate,
until we tracked their entrance,
never speaking the word aloud
because something lurks in
the attic eaves of the creature's name
we preferred not to articulate –
and maybe all atrocity starts there,
a well of blood wrath and myth
atrophied to superstition
beneath the mortar of language
we use to describe the world.
At any rate we wanted them dead,
poured in half a quart of poison,

ratcheted the orifice shut
with a metal grate.

SEVEN THINGS ABOUT STEPHANIE

1
She isn't a morning person

2
Her wounded voice outside,
its small bruise of outrage –
three more casualties
in the flower box this morning,
nothing deters the goddamn squirrels

Such a small thing,
she doesn't know why
it makes her feel so
defenceless

3
Every morning her ex would stand
at the bedroom window
proclaiming the glories of the day
before he'd even had a coffee,
he thought it might rub off on her eventually

His back to the room
as he held the curtains wide,
his bare buttocks like
two sad loaves in a pan

4
Press clippings from Palestine on the table,
three years of work in a shoebox –
suicide bombings, racist Israeli soccer players,
bodies strewn in a Jewish market,
flesh desecrated by the torn flesh
of watermelon

Deadpan staccato of her reporter's voice:
Hero of Intifada Imprisoned by Palestinian Authority
Mideast Peace Deal in Jeopardy

5
Her ex checks in every morning, early,
the calls inevitable and wrenching,
his passion relentless as the squirrels
raiding her morning glories,
their brazen clicking
laughter

6
Back from the phone,
an air of heightened security
about her, checkpoints,
roadblocks

Questions bloom on the fringe
of headlines, official sources,
circle the room like flowered wallpaper,
omnipresent, all but invisible

Who owns a life?

What makes us
what we are?

7
Her question:
"All I want are some flowers on the deck,
is that too much to ask?"

Blood meal in the soil
will keep squirrels away from the bulbs –
but that isn't the answer
she's looking for

ENTROPY

Look up, look waaay up –
static constellations, illusion of permanence

Night sky stares back like a face
through a car window,
star-pocked darkness a cold breath
in the expanding lung of space

Love is a little more complicated
but beauty is just an accident
of physics

Light driving hard through darkness
long after its star succumbs
to exhaustion,
but not even light will escape
the lag of the universe,
the weight of pure energy
congealing into loss

Entropy, I know the meaning of the word
though the precise definition escapes me,
bowed wheel of the solar system
buckling under its own heft,
blossoming absence –

Some day our star will collapse
why should our lives be
any different

THE MATH

In Storrington Township
north of Kingston,
roadside houses cast

pale planes of light from
kitchen windows,
old barns tilt acutely

in the dark fields,
falling so slowly they seem
motionless.

A racoon crossing pavement
stalls in the headlights
like someone caught cheating

and the car does the math,
insisting what can't be
prevented is necessary.

If we come to any truth
we come to it
by accident alone.

FOG CITY

Running the Quidi Vidi loop in mauzy weather,
alone on the trail but for the vague outline of
a retriever trotting ahead,
arc of the tail's baton marking time.
A ballgame on the diamond at Caribou Field,
gauzy park lights visible on the opposite shore –
blunted *chink* of the metal bat making contact,
muffled commotion as a pop fly
disappears into grey-mesh sky,
teammates calling advice on distance,
direction, index fingers extended
pointlessly toward absence.
The one silent player is the outfielder
judging the ball's arc by its trajectory
as it leaves the bat
and I can feel the contours of
his solitude clear across the lake,
a loneliness made worse by company,
by the encouragement of others.

That edgeless shape of a dog
steadily ahead on the trail
and not appearing to belong to anyone.

EMERGENCY ROADSIDE ASSISTANCE

I decide to walk
alongside the river. It's the kind of night
that brings men and rivers close.
         – Raymond Carver

Halfway along the back roads
to Ottawa the car stalls,
rolls to a stop on
the highway shoulder.
The engine gurgles and dies,
gurgles and dies
until it's helplessly flooded.
The high beams of occasional vehicles
pulse in the rear-view
before they stream past.
Nothing for miles
in both directions but the stars.
No telling how far
I'll have to go to find
a phone tonight and I sit here
frosting the windshield as
the last of the light goes under,
thinking about that.

The truth is I don't have
the heart for poetry
much these days,
a body is more comfort,
the ancient animal heat of it,

a river has more to say
about love and time
and the two or three other things
in the world that can't be helped.
That bitter walk in the cold
ahead of me, for instance.
Blue shadow of snow
drifting in the roadside grass,
a moon just rising
on the dark tide.

THE LATE MACBETH

His body divorced him slowly
like a flock of birds leaving
a wire, one set of wings at a time –
still in sight, but past retrieving.

Extremities first, his right foot
dropping asleep, forcing a limp
until the left faltered numb,
conspiring to abort every step.

Fingers and tongue deadened, as if
wrapped in a muffle of feather down –
each affliction painless and shameful,
like a ship run aground in sand.

His infant child seemed to chase him,
her development a mirror
image of his progressive loss;
her wonder, reversed, his terror.

Still, he got on with things, wrote
the last poems, read. Tried to swallow
the panic that galled his throat,
never mentioned the dream of crows.

After his voice abandoned him
his wife scissored an alphabet
and they relearned the grace of words:
letters raised like a wick, and lit.

At the end he was stripped of all
but that fire, its sad, splendid
glow. When his wife offered him
the sedative they knew would end it

he asked "How long will I sleep?"
spelled it out, letter by letter.
The fear had left them both by then.
She told him, "Until you're better."

STATIC

Shuck my clothes in the dark.
Blue sparks click in
the charged fabric as I peel
a sweatshirt over my head
and a close-up of Mom and Dad
at the kitchen sink flickers by,
two brace of rabbit
on the counter for skinning –
I wasn't old enough to wield the knife,
watched the blade bracelet
the back paws, muffler of fur
jacked off the carcass,
stripped clear of the head

The stink of blood and offal
always drove me outside
but there was something beautiful
about the bared machinery
of those bodies,
grain of muscle taut
as guy wire over bone;
only the delicate fur cuffs
at the paw-tips made them
seem unfortunate,
and I've never felt so naked
going to bed alone as now,
picturing those cadavers
laid against porcelain,
the flesh dark as cedar

Shake out my clothes once more
for the comforting chatter
of static in the material,
its brief constellation of light

NORTHERN ONTARIO: BERRY PICKING

The bushes grow over a grey wreckage
of stone near marshland,
clear summer air singed by
keening blackflies, mosquitoes.
Canopies of green leaves
camouflage the berries
where they grow close to the earth,
most of them touched by the first frost –
small blue bouquets scarred black,
skin tearing as they're pulled
free from stems,
bruising our fingers with their fragility.
We drop them into quart baskets
at our feet or stain our mouths
with their darkness.

Semicircle of poplar guards the clearing,
leaves fringed with autumn's yellow caution,
already anticipating a cold flood of snow,
the long winter song of absence,
while the last surf of summer heat
breaks on the stones where we stoop –
heat still tart enough to burn
the bare skin of our necks,
that bittersweetness.

Two months from now
this will be a different country.

The cold stirred us from sleep when
the wood stove's busy tick wound down
to embers bled of warmth, their smoulder
faint as the light of distant stars and
our bodies under the dead weight of
comforters unable to hold the fire's heat.
I'd leave you then, feeling my way
to the woodbox in the pitch,
stoking the coals to catch a length
of dry birch or spruce,
my breath in the stove's mouth
raising a red glow like a flag,
a thin tongue of flame sudden
as a struck match taking in the bark.

Cloudless outside, and still,
clarity of the night sky above
the lake like a niggling unnamed fear
thrown into sudden, sharp relief.
A white lamp of frost lighting
the path to the car, my footsteps
on packed snow an audible ache,
an oddly distorted heartbeat.
The motor spat and fizzled
like green wood over kindling
before kicking into a cranky blaze,
and I sat waiting for winter to burn
out of the cylinders, picturing you
asleep beside the new fire:

a stray flanker lighting on bare skin,
a weightless singe.

The small sacrifices I offered through
those bitter nights, my vigils nursing
an engine through the cold, intended to
console us both for the larger failure.
The fire I recovered from darkness
meant to hold your body in warmth
and sleep a few hours longer.
To comfort you after I'd gone.

ARSON

She thought it was summer rain that woke her,
lay listening to the wavering spit and clatter
through the open window, lifted her head
to a blank television screen surging crimson –
the old carriage house in the yard set alight
and hemorrhaging red through broken panes,
a storey of angry flame standing above the shingles.

I toured the gutted wreck next morning –
a fibreglass kayak curdled like a piece
of discarded chewing gum, a stored
chesterfield gnawed to the raw metal frame.
She stood outside with a coffee, calm,
one more familiar thing stripped
from her life, part of the bleeding
she's come to expect of the world.

Everywhere I stepped in the ruined building
the treads of my shoes stood out
in the soot like fingerprints.

NORTHERN ONTARIO: FINNISH CEMETERY

Mortared stone at the entrance,
rows of unbordered gravesites
bordered by a narrow band of spruce.
In the wilt of afternoon heat
her father walks ahead with the mower,
his long complicated silence buried
in the sloppy growl of the engine
while she follows behind,
her scythe taking down the waist-high
purple lupins around her grandfather's grave.

Finnish names chiselled into marble,
words the country has never learned
to speak properly –
Koske, Heikeilla, Ilyjuki –
this century's immigrants, arriving
to clear a piece of land with an axe
and the strength of a body that knows
it can't go home.
Some gave up hope in the end,
broken by root-bound fields and
the long darkness of winters that
guttered speech into stoic silence;
bones of the first settlers another knot
in the stubborn tangle
of earth.

Someday she knows she will bury her father
where the oiled blade sings neatly

through the green stalks,
and there is so much she'd like to hear
from him, so much she wants to have said
before he is lain here
like a length of summer grass.

A father can be a love as difficult
as an adopted country,
part of him always remains a stranger.
She follows behind him now because
she has nowhere else to go,
because the summers here are brief.
Moves in his shadow,
thinking about silence, about
the scythe, about the purple lupins
fallen around her feet.

THE QUICK

Leech in shallow water,
three inches of appetite riding currents
like a weed where the girls wade barefoot
near the shore, a trick of the light
severing their legs below the knees.

After the screaming and the shaken salt
they refuse to go back in the lake,
there's too much life hidden in it.

Bird at the foot of the cottage window,
neck broken by clouds in
its mirrored face.

An architecture so delicate,
so much like themselves, the girls refuse
to think it a dead thing –

cradle the candle-flame of its body,
turning it in the afternoon sunlight
to stir the feathers' iridescence.

We dig a shallow grave
among the roots of a tree,
they crown it with a tiara of stones.

At night they turn in their beds
as stars nettle their foreheads
against the dark,
each thorn of light a raw ache
like pulling a hangnail to the quick.

The lake's blank face
mirrors them back as if everything
beneath its surface was motionless,
still.

BUSHED

On Round Lake, two hours north of North Bay

Cool July night, sodden grey tarp of cloud.
Beneath raggedly tiered rows of trees
we surrender shoes and light summer clothes.
Lisp of wind in the wet thatch of leaves
like the rustling of a waiting audience.
Count to three before rushing the chill,
whisky-cold kissing us everywhere at once –
our stunned voices skim the water's palm
and sink into darkness like skipped stones.

Part of what you are leaks into the country
and gets lost out here. The country fills
you up with strangeness. Woods whispering on
for miles, but it feels like depth, not distance –
no wonder lone settlers found something willed
in all this silence that stripped their minds,
plunged them naked into bottomless bush.

The lake's raw whisker of frost bristles
against our skin. Somewhere far beneath us
muscled stars of splake and pickerel
navigate a current of human voices.
On shore the light of fireflies flash –
Morse code broken in the underbrush.

FINNISH CEMETERY REVISITED

We walk in above the fence like
spirits about to leave the world,
our tracks a darkness in snowdrifts behind us.
30 below, and still, the ghost of each breath
a clean shirt on a clothesline.
Cold light of stars needling the night sky like
feeling returning to a numb hand.

At the gravesite Wanda kneels
to clear the headstone,
her father lights a candle inside a jar.
Under our feet his mother's body gutters
in the last darkness a body knows,
his father beside her already smoke.
Their names shadow and flicker
in the yellow glow of the wick.

It's the living that haunt the homes
of the dead, wanting something
from them we can't articulate,
something we can only gesture dumbly towards.
Spruce trees circle the graveyard
with a quiet that could be taken for patience,
the moon stares through branches, pale
as a face of the recently dead.
Even the stars overhead
have been touched by the frost.

ARTIFACTS

An old couple lived here before you and I.
Brother and sister, raised in this house,
forced home after years away
by a stingy pension, the death of a spouse.

They didn't get on at all in the end,
the neighbours say, led separate lives,
divided the six rooms between them,
ate separate meals at appointed times.

Stuffed in a drawer, we found sheets of paper
columned with scores, their names scrawled at the top –
they must have argued over words for years
till first the Scrabble, then the talking stopped.

A sad story told by sad artifacts
we never thought might spell out our own.
A house divided as if split by an axe.
Two people sitting to their meals alone.

BELONGINGS

I wanted the only life that is mine,
took back the words of an old promise
and folded them away in a drawer

like clothes suited to another season,
but there are nights I revisit that street
just for the warmth

of her shaded lights in the windows,
the walnut tree shielding the veranda
from the cold eyes of stars.

Everything looks at home
beneath those branches now,
a flowering quilt of clematis

stitched to the trellis, her cat asleep
on the lawn by the walkway,
each blade of grass a rough tongue

licking its dreams smooth.
The white house sits still as
a vessel at anchor, the lighted rooms

emptied of my belongings.

Our last night
together in that house
I held your hand through
three hours of the Scots
betraying themselves
to the English
and left it at that.

You knelt to interrupt
the credits as they rolled
on the screen.

Pressed *Rewind*.

RETURNING

First storm of a late winter, heavy
snow, wind driven by the weight
of human anticipation,
our resignation to the season's
turning.

At the table this morning,
the window behind you haloed
with storm phosphorescence,
naked trees so graceful in white,
their branches tapping the glass.
Furnace murmuring beneath
kitchen warmth like the voice
of the child I did not want,
and you saying *I know
you aren't coming home.*
Your face in that
light, how it changed you.

It's our helplessness we keep
returning to, the seasons swinging
in our blood.
Love as inevitable
as inadequate and vice versa,
every beautiful thing shadowed by sadness.
Winter reaching for us as we sat
together at the kitchen table,
high windows bleeding

invisible veins of heat
into the storm.

NORTHERN LIGHTS, LOOKING BACK

We waded out into the damp air
to watch those enormous seines of light,
delicate mesh moored to the constant stars,
their drift and settle miming tides.

Standing beneath them we both felt stripped,
ambushed by awe and strangely heartsick –
cold and alone and lost in their wake
like two dim stars the sky had dropped.

The hard times were anchored miles off still –
it was just beauty that hooked and held our sight,
made us lonely for something that travelled
through our time like water sieving a net.

I didn't think to turn to watch your face
but, looking back, I wish I had. Our lives then
lit by the pitch of the sky's blind grace,
until night leant down to draw the light in.

THE PROJECT

If I was born to the grain
and resin of language
worked in solitude,
to hours sealing cracks
with putty and sawdust,
I was born to this as well –
days when it seems perfectly
pointless, architecture of failure,
half a house of cards
any stray breeze could ruin.

This afternoon I say
fuck it, go soak my head
in the claw-foot tub tucked
under fourth-floor rafters,
feeling defeated, relieved,
distant traffic filtering through
a placenta of water.

Before the bath goes cold I hear
the creak of the neighbour's taps –
our bathrooms separated
by an ancient red-brick wall,
sinews of light passing through
porous mortar with the drone
of conversation and
running water, fragrance
of bath oil, shampoo.

For months I've overheard
them talking gibberish
to their first child, listened
to her monosyllabic complaints
as they dribbled water
over her hair,
her voice wobbling, comic,
like a newborn's oversized head
on the milky-green stalk of its spine.

Today she's speaking
her first blunt unfinished words,
a barely conscious repetition
like hammering nails,
Mamma, she says, *Dada*.
She can just contain her enthusiasm,
working the snug hinge
of the consonants,
slapping the water to punctuate
each declaration.
Something in her demands it.

Something sends me
naked to my desk
to write this down.

THE NAKED MAN

Shower room's peace shattered by boys launched
like rockets, their racket sudden as rain
on a tin roof. Shyness sharp as a sprain
makes him wince at the sight of his paunch,

his penis crouched in its thicket of curls.
But the boys ignore the naked man beside
them, their voices pitched toward registers
beyond hearing, skin translucent white,

everything about them in ascendance,
inching toward their adult heights
without hesitation or reluctance.
They orbit his silence like satellites

trailing the dead weight of stars –
there's no way to warn them what lies ahead
and he's torn by a father's helpless regret,
seeing them so unguarded, so free of scars.

ROADKILL

Tawny summer evening late last June,
living-room windows inlaid with gold leaf,
sunlight drawing blood to the skin
of strawberries in the garden.

His four-year-old mind miming a vortex
of crows over roadkill,
my nephew circled the house
in search of his father,
the childish symmetry of his face lost
to the weight of a question born with him
and suddenly articulate in his mind
like a riddle of blank spaces
set alight with letters.

Dad, he said, *when I die, is that forever?*
This from a child unable to count
in sequence beyond ten.

Yes, Matthew, my brother told him,
slow train snaking into a car
stalled at the crossing,
that's forever.

The day still two half-hour game shows
from dusk, Matthew went to bed,
skipping *Wheel of Fortune* at 7:30,
refusing even the stories
his father offered to read.

My brother lay with him
long after he fell asleep,
stroking the skin of his back,
tracing the delicate curve of the spine,
because physical comfort is all
we can take from the world
when the day falls prey to carrion fact.

The boy's breath rose and fell beside him,
sweet as a field of fresh-mown clover.

She was uncharacteristically late
and they both fought a sense of wild
dread, the certainty of her condition
filling their heads like the feedback hum
of an amplifier overheating.
Nothing for it but surrender to fate –
they sat wringing their hands, debating
names for the inevitable child.

She was a year older and did him
the favour of feigning disbelief
when he confessed she was his first.
Two kids in love: he'd have proposed
and she'd have said yes, for better or worse,
if it hadn't ended with the sudden relief
of menstrual blood staining her clothes.

Years later it came to him second-hand,
she'd married and had a son,
that both nearly died during the birth:
the baby obstructed, a long delay
in utero starving him of oxygen.
It was chance that either survived
and the damage to the child's brain
meant he'd never manage to hold
a fork, or take an uncomplicated breath.

Heard nothing more till he was told
she lost her son at the age of five.
He didn't even know the boy's name.

He's almost given up on you, sleeper,
on the part of himself that imagines
nuzzling the fat pink erasers of your feet,
thinks of nursing bruises at your temples
where the forceps would have coaxed
the greedy flame of your voice into
his cupped and waiting hands.
His selfishness is the spell that holds you
submerged like a lost child in a fairy tale,
your absence ripening on the branches of
these words like orchard fruit,
and his mouth on his lover's body
so close to the place you would stir
startles him with nostalgia and loneliness,
like hearing the old stories in which
a beautiful sleeper is woken with a kiss.
He troubles you now like any father,
haunted by his failures, wanting
forgiveness for loving you only as well
as his weaknesses allowed, for turning
his back when he might have touched
his lips to your dreaming face,
watched your eyes startle open
on the brightly candled stage of your life.

Communion

At the end of every visit,
his car polished and packed for home,
my grandfather stood in the kitchen
and bribed my brothers and I to swear,
holding a silver coin like the Catholic host
above our kneeling figures while
he lead us through a liturgy
of profanity:

> Say *God Damn.*
> Say *Jesus Christ.*
> Say *Sonofabitch.*

Still children when he died,
we aped the grief around us
just as we'd cursed for him,
bawling when the congregation
rose to sing its sad Methodist hymns,
swallowing the salt of our tears
when the minister spoke over
the lowered coffin, gravel rattling
off the polished lid –
it was mysterious and melancholy
and strangely unaffecting at the time.

The quarters were our excuse
but it was those words we wanted,

their metallic shimmer,
permission to speak beyond our years
in our mother's disapproving presence.
Their aftertaste like that salt scald
of grief in our mouths,
its slow lingering burn.

Pathetic Fallacy

All day October rain,
their breath smoking the air
like the breath of horses
in pictures from the old country,
the storm pelting the shingle roof
where they stood for shelter
near the graveyard.
Her feet numb in unfamiliar black shoes
and she shifted and stamped
on the concrete floor to bring
the feeling back to them.

Ten years old,
she doesn't remember crying,
thought all funerals were accompanied
by clouds dark as a hearse,
her Oma dead and whispering
in the grey stampede of rain,
the ache in her feet like
an offering to the weather's grief.
Every detail seemed preordained
and necessary, the bitter cold,

the mourners stabled together
in the tiny shack,
and no one speaking
over the steady clop of the rain
as it ran through the streets
and carried the old woman
away.

FEVER

Big Island Cemetery, Prince Edward County, Ontario

Most of the headstones have long since collapsed,
moss and a tangled mesh of grasses obscuring
the carefully wrought names and dates,
the chiselled Victorian pieties,
trite and sadly implausible a century on.

Several clusters of marble testament to
a minor calamity that passed through
Loyalist country in 1885 and 86,
some indiscriminate disease moving from
family to family like a slash-and-burn
homesteader clearing brush,
old and young alike twisting in their beds
as if turning on a spit,
their senses so addled by fever
they didn't recognize the people
who tended them as they died.
When those who'd nursed the dead
took sick themselves, their heads were
scorched clean of the names and faces
they'd hardly had time to mourn.

How ancient those lives seem now,
ravaged and almost past remembering:
even God struggles to untangle the skein
of their voices from the stars,
to recall the simple clarity of prayers

that kept them awake at night,
their faces in lamplight dazzled with tears.
Barely a hundred years of forgetting in this field
and time beyond time to carry on forgetting,
and being forgotten.

Everyone these people once cared for is dead
and they haven't so much as turned in their beds.

LOOM

Burnt Woods Cemetery, Western Bay, Newfoundland

The meadow grass hemming
the gravesites is coarse as raw wool,
thickets of dry thistle
stand like needles clustered
in a pincushion; overhead
a shoddy bolt of cloud
gone ragged at the edges.

Headstones facing the Atlantic,
set in rows like figures being
fitted by a tailor;
six feet beneath them
the remains of the cloth I was cut from,
the patterns lifted to cobble
my features together.

Such a slow undressing –
bones divested of flesh,
purposeless and absurd,
like a dressmaker's dummy
relegated to the basement;
skulls hollow as thimbles,
picked clean of every thread
of memory, design.

They were born into times
when you made do,

stitched trousers out of burlap sacking,
salvaged skirts from a wreck
of worn curtains,
when there was no disguising
most of a life comes to us piecemeal,
second-hand.

Even the love I bear these strangers
is makeshift, threadbare,
fashioned by necessity.
The bitter cold draws thin gloves
of blood to my hands
and I follow the footpath
weaving among their graves
as long as I can stand the keen,
surrender them finally to the wind
shearing in off the endless
grey loom of the sea.

SCAVENGER'S DIARY

After she's been settled for the night
he runs the loop around Quidi Vidi Lake,
hoping to catch sight of the fox
that once crossed the road
down to the old village
and stopped to stare back at him,
eyes in the steady strobe of headlights
like the clock flashing on a VCR.

He sits at his mother's sewing table
in the basement, coffee mug
bristling with pens,
a dull circle of lamplight
where he writes:

> *the fox loped into tuckamore and alder,*
> *its scent on the bare branches*
> *a wild patience*

Each morning he washes her back
while his mother rubs lotion into the sores
that are stripping away the flesh
above the tailbone.
The old woman watches him adjust
the pillow beneath her head,
suspicion clouding her eyes:

his name has already abandoned her,
the taste of partridgeberries,
the smell of falling snow.

While she sleeps
he writes:

> *end of November,*
> *afternoon light so weak now*
> *darkness is almost a relief*

And:

> *blood blisters rose on her heels*
> *like stigmata,*
> *lidless pupils,*
> *their blind stare*

His mother calls him upstairs
to help turn her, and he leaves
the notebook open on the desk,
words nudging the air with
wet, delicate nostrils.
When he comes back to the page
the smell of her skin is a shadow
his hands cast in the lamplight.

Every day his appetite for the work increases
although he refuses to name
what moves him *hunger*.

    love, he writes.

    love

SIMMER

All her life my grandmother loved dusk,
the ambiguity of twilight,
how darkness seemed to seep
from the earth,
street lamps flickering
to life while clouds shone
and blushed on the horizon
like apples ripening on a windowsill.

A watched pot never boils,
she used to tell us,
as if emotional truth
could be winnowed
from the husk of cold fact.

After the funeral we followed the hearse
in through the country to Twillingate,
crossing the causeways that replaced
ferries in the 70s, islands
strung on an asphalt necklace.
Darkness falling early,
cold December rain.

I remember the line of vehicles
up the hill from the old ferry dock
those summer afternoons
we drove out to visit,
my brothers and I shirtless
and simmering in the back seat.
All gravel highway at the time,
the windshield and dashboard
shimmering with road-dust.
Sunlight hammering the metal roofs
of the cars made us
miserable with waiting.

I tried not to watch for the boat.

DARKNESS TURNS

A year later the old woman's deathbed
sleeps a boy home for the holidays,
a poinsettia stowed in her closet to stain
the green leaves a seasonal red.
Spruce tree starred in a string of coloured lights
down the hall, a table weighted with food,
with fruitcake dark and heavy as stone.

Relentless winter: the driveway muscled clean
each morning is buried again at night,
flesh so racked with shovelling the grey mind burns,
the stricken body forgets what it was.
Go at the old questions with the same
dogged effort, scrape the blade down to bone –
it all drifts in while our eyes are closed.
No one remembers why darkness turns
the green poinsettia red. It just does.

WATER BIRDS: A LETTER

That April afternoon two waterfowl
crossed a lake still bordered with ice,
their calls part Chaplin waddle, part wail;
trees on the far shore turned the cries
inside-out to echo them back to us
and it was good to be there, Julie,
surrounded by the disorder of spring,
the sun's unfamiliar surge like the heat
of a stoked furnace, wind off the water
like postcards from January.

I used to think of happiness as
the absence of grief or regret,
saw emotions as separate states
we moved through like the seasons.
But the surface ice resists every inch
of its inevitable erasure,
the deepest part of the lake will
survive August still dreaming of frost.
All winter the rock we sat against
rooted the spare heat of its lichen and moss
and it's true no measure of content
could make me love my life
as fiercely as learning to live with loss.

Last year I'd have missed something here
and only echo it from a distance still –
two birds mirrored over the water,
their voices almost identical.

BLUE IN GREEN (TAKE 2)

Hungover this morning
and slightly stoned on allergy pills,
I'm navigating a section of bright
countryside just north of nausea,
Bill Evans at his mellowest holding
the road map and probably wrecked
as he played the black and tan melody,
all ten fingers intent as bees
drunk on honey sweetness.

Spring again, every green thing
slurring pollen into the blue
like a party of name-droppers
intoxicated by its own gossip,
the buzz of life in the air
so thick it's nearly audible.

The music makes me feel clumsy
with my time, it drifts off the map
without ever losing its way,
chords polished and carefully placed
like stones marking a path home,
like notes I'd like to write to myself:

You are exactly where you need to be.

Pay attention to everything.

It's good to be alive.

BLUE IN GREEN (TAKE 3)

Hungover this morning
and slightly stoned on
allergy pills,
I'm chasing the blue shade
of Bill Evans's hands
to keep the bright at bay,
music filtering sunlight
like a deep pool of water.

Julie turns toward me to say
I always wake up
thinking about food or sex
and this time of year
the world offers endless
improvisations on those themes.
Hard to explain jazz
or addiction with a notion
as simple as appetite,
but those variations
inhabit its frequency
the same as blue does green.

The music meadows the late hours
of the morning,
each note has the heft,
the pendulous grace of
bees in flight –
too heavy for their wings,

they're kept aloft by desire,
by their hunger for life.

NAKED

All day wrestling half a poem
content to live that way,
I leave it awhile to rest my back,
wander my two small rooms
as the day slowly runs out of fuel,
bright ribbon of exhaust
rimming the horizon

Nothing ends the way we intend –
I've fallen in love for the last time
twice already,
reason is no match for
the appetites of the heart

Run a bath and lie back,
the heat drawing a flush to my skin
the way I'd like the last lines
of that poem to come,
sunset, credits scrawled in scarlet,
the kind of closure the body
doesn't survive

Love and poetry, meaning –
maybe it's just stubborn animal machinery
manufacturing light for the mind
with darkness at the door

THE DIFFERENCE

He wakes early in a friend's apartment,
lying in the exact same posture
he settled into seven hours before,
turns his head slowly to place himself,
disoriented by borrowed space, realizes
he's slept all night without dreaming.

Watery April light, the dampness in it on
the hardwood underfoot as he scrounges
for teabags in the unfamiliar kitchen,
alone but not lonely, as if it were possible
to choose one and not the other.

The kettle stirred by
a barely perceptible tremor
just before it boils.

A good place to start over, he thinks,
although he couldn't name his location
or fix it on a map of his life.
Four open cartons of milk in the fridge,
all but one past their *best before* date.
Two bowls, one sugar, one salt,
beside the teapot on the counter,
no way to tell the difference
but to taste them both.

AFTER THE FACT

A voice reported the weather but she missed it. She didn't know it was the weather until it was gone.

– Don DeLillo

It was a dream she described to him,
embarrassed and in love with it
at the same time, how she lay
naked under lamplight as he wrote
a poem on her skin,
letters rising on her belly and thighs
like a palimpsest,
like something beautiful within her
his hand was simply tracing
as it came to the surface.

She brought it up before they made love
or in the drift afterwards,
joking about body paint in a way
so understated he never thought of it
as suggestion or request,
though her shyness mirrored his own
when he asked her to read
a new story or poem,
before things ended between them.

Long after the fact, he tried
to write it for her, and failed,
the words she'd imagined like
a dream defying morning logic,

so far beyond him he could only register
their growing bewilderment –
how they stepped onto their balconies at dusk
to taste the day's weather
and watch stars surface in the dark,
each troubled by a beauty
they were meant to articulate
and never would

how it was almost there
before it was lost for good.

THE NARROWS

Days without rain he wakes to hammers
stammering somewhere in the cramped warren
of yards behind his house, hair at the back
of his neck rising to the complaint of nails
being pried from old lumber, the squeal
as they're uprooted an inch at a time
almost human.

A view of the Narrows from his bedroom,
he spends part of each day staring out at
the North Atlantic framed by the harbour's
stone cliffs, trying to name the *something*
about the ocean that compels and terrifies him.
Relentless pendulum of the tides maybe,
the secret worlds carouselling in those cold fathoms.

Evenings he sits in darkness, watching men
and women in lighted rooms across the street,
guessing at their thoughts, at the irreducible truth
of their lives moving just under the surface
of what he can see, the way they turn suddenly
and tilt their heads to one side, listening.

Falls asleep at night with the ocean breathing outside
his window, all around him the imperceptible hum
of people settling in the hive of the city.
Still a stranger to every one of them.

VIEW OF THE MOON FROM THE DECK
BUILT ABOVE HIS KITCHEN

Constructed by some amateur unconcerned
with the finer details of carpentry, with consequences,
joists laid a foot too wide so the boards bow
beneath the weight of a body, the corner posts
sunk into the roof and poorly sealed with pitch,
ceiling plaster blistered by rainwater seeping
through leaks too insidious to trace,
and no hope of putting it right without taking
the whole goddamn thing down.

The moon nearly full across the harbour,
blue weight of the Southside Hills bowed
in darkness beneath it.

The rain getting in.

He took his shift that night to keep company
with her dying, her breath clotted with fluid,
heart treading water in the cavity of her chest,
one hand flailing like a distress signal
he could only watch from his impossible distance.
Before dawn she vomited a mouthful
of black bile and left them to the morning's
muffled light gathering at the windows.

He watched from the doorway as a doctor
unpacked her stethoscope, surprised to register
her loveliness, the pulse of it brimming his head
as she nodded in time to the nothing she heard
of the stilled heart, as she scrawled a florid,
illegible signature on the Certificate of Death.
The shrouded body strapped to a stretcher then
and wheeled through rain to the hearse,
black car drifting off into the raw mouth
of December weather, leaving them
to strip the bed, scour the soiled sheets.

A long dirty morning and no relief from it
but his time in the presence of the lovely doctor
when he was unfaithful to a fresh grief,
ashamed of the infidelity, and grateful to see
the beautiful survives what he will not.

CHAPEL STREET TORQUE

Across the street from his new house
the church has been abandoned
by God, converted to condos
with a view of the harbour,
values ratcheted above
two hundred grand apiece
by civil servants and lawyers
and oil money leeching
into the downtown core

The cheap apartments and
rooming houses on either side
of him cling to the hill
like barnacles to a ship's hull;
buddy next door scatters stale bread
into the road to watch
pigeons fight,
three and four at a time
descending in tight circles
around a mouldy crust
like bathwater running
down a drain

Each day turns with the same
irresistible torque,
the street's steep grade tugging
like the undertow of a surf
as it falls away to the harbour,
the simple act of holding on

corkscrewing him deeper
into whatever life it is
he's chosen here

All night the harbour light
fixed to the chapel spire shines
down the Narrows to thread ships
through shoal water, sunkers –
his rooms submarined by
its luminous blue
like a place anointed,
like a home improbably blessed

HIS CENTURY

Sometime before light
the bed shakes him out of sleep –
second time in a month,
a shudder through the frame,
the *tic-tic-tic* of the lamp
rocking on the nightstand,
the house quivering
in the wake of a passing train.

There is no train.

He listens hard in the dark,
quieting his breath to register
the cycle of vibrations,
intimate and steady
and seeming to arrive from
a long way off.

Ten minutes of whispered motion
before stillness settles,
he lies awake considering
lame possibilities,
wind or late night traffic,
the refrigerator chugging quietly
two floors down,
the idiosyncrasies of a house
built a hundred years ago.

How many people conceived
in these rooms, he wonders,
how many have died here?
A century teeming in the darkness,
untold lives still travelling the outskirts
of his own, and he lies still,
wanting them to pass undisturbed.

He is a long time getting
back to sleep.

THE COME-ON

A long sultry day turns
its attention to the horizon,
flirting casually with darkness

The light outside the window
slips into something
more comfortable

The warmth of the sun almost down
like a mouth on the bare nape
of his neck

The evening's first star
a solitary beauty mark
on the sky's blue shoulder

It's night coming on
and knowing he will never hold it
that makes the world so seductive

The star's loneliness
makes it seem
the one perfect thing

ACKNOWLEDGEMENTS

The poems in the middle section of this book are for Wanda.

"Water Birds," "After the Fact," and several other poems in the last third of the book (you know the ones) are for J.

Support from the Canada Council for the Arts and the Ontario Arts Council made the writing of much of this book possible.

The lyric quoted in "Jar of Blues" is from the song "This Is Hip," written by John Lee Hooker. Copyright © 1991 by Boogie One Music (BMI)/Administered by Bug Music, Inc., Los Angeles. All rights reserved. Used by permission.

The epigraph to the poem "Emergency Roadside Assistance" is from the poem "Cutlery," from *Ultramarine* by Raymond Carver. Copyright © 1986 by Raymond Carver. Reprinted by permission of International Creative Management Inc.

The epigraph to "After the Fact" is from *The Body Artist* by Don DeLillo. Copyright © 2001 by Don DeLillo. Reprinted with the permission of Scribner, a division of Simon & Schuster, Inc.

A selection of the poems included here appeared as a Trout Lily Press chapbook, *Emergency Roadside Assistance* (2001). Thanks to TLP for the beautiful book and to Gary Draper for his emergency roadside editorial assistance.

97

Earlier versions of many of these pieces were first published in *Arc*, *Descant*, *The Fiddlehead*, *The Malahat Review*, *The New Quarterly*, and *TickleAce*.

A slightly different version of "Northern Ontario: Finnish Cemetery" appeared in *Arguments with Gravity*, published by Quarry Press in 1996.

Alison Pick has been first reader of most of the poems I've written in the last two years and she suggested many improvements, some of which I had the good sense to incorporate.

Stan Dragland edited the entire manuscript. Every poem in the book sat up and paid attention when he walked into the room. I thank him for his hobnailed boots and hope he's enjoying the Scotch.